Baby's First Steps in Spanish

ERIKA LEVY,

WITH A CHAPTER BY ELIZABET

EDITOR: ZVJEZDANA VRZIĆ, PH.D.

LIVING LANGUAGE®
A Random House Company

Copyright © 2001 by Living Language, A Random House Company

The diagram of the mouth courtesy of *Random House Webster's College Dictionary*
Copyright © 2000 by Random House, Inc.

Published by Living Language, A Random House Company, New York, New York.
Living Language is a member of the Random House Information Group.

Random House, Inc. New York, Toronto, London, Sydney, Auckland

www.livinglanguage.com

Printed in Mexico.

Designed by Barbara Balch

Library of Congress Cataloging-in-Publication Data available

ISBN 0-609-60740-5

10 9 8 7 6 5 4 3

First Paperback Edition

À MA MÈRE, VALERIE LEVY, AND
FOR MY FATHER, ALAN LEVY,
FOR THEIR INFINITE LOVE
AND MULTILINGUAL IMPRINTING

Author's Acknowledgments

Many thanks to Random House's Living Language staff: Zviezdana Verzich, Christopher Warnasch, Ana Stojanović, and Eric Sommer, for making this book possible. Great thanks also to Dr. Loraine K. Obler and Dr. Winifred Strange at the City University of New York's Graduate Center for their expertise. Special thanks to Monica Levy, Valerie Levy, Alan Levy, Lisa Keloufi, Mélina Keloufi, Joël Keloufi, and Lionel Borée for their help with the music, poetry, and prose. Special thanks also to Mira Goral, Craig Hetzer, Helen Langone, and Philip Yanowitch for their sacrifices during this critical period for book-writing.

Contents

Introduction to the Package

Baby's First Steps in Spanish offers your baby sounds of a foreign language during a critical period in her linguistic development.[1] Your baby will be enchanted by soothing Spanish songs, poems, rhymes, and words as she naturally absorbs Spanish speech sounds and intonations. You will take pleasure in your baby's extraordinary linguistic feats. By reading this book, you will also discover how and why your baby does so effortlessly what may seem so difficult to you.

THE PREMISE

*O*ur product is research-based, resting on state-of the-art knowledge from the fields of infant speech perception, speech pathology, language acquisition, and multilingualism. Research has shown that humans are born with the ability to distinguish all the possible sounds of the world's languages. Thus newborns all over the world have no problem hearing the difference between the French *u* sound (like English *oo*) in *vous* "you" and the *ü* sound in *vue* "view." On the other hand, this slight sound difference may not be heard by adults who speak English, which has no such similar sound distinctions.

Important changes in your baby's perceptual abilities occur toward the second half of her first year of life. During this period, babies

---

[1]To refer to your baby, the generic *he* and *she* will be alternated among chapters of the book, in fairness to boys and girls.

grow attuned to the sounds of the language or languages in their surroundings, and lose the ability to distinguish other, foreign sounds they were able to perceive just a few months earlier. Ten-month-old infants surrounded by English have as much difficulty distinguishing the French *u* and *ü* sounds as you do if English is your only language. Young children surrounded by Japanese no longer hear the difference between the *l* sound and the *r* sound because Japanese does not make use of this sound distinction. When sounds do not exist in the languages of their environment, babies will lose their ability to perceive them.

Fast forward to adulthood. When speakers don't have correct, "native-like" perception of the sounds of a language, they won't be able to pronounce them accurately. Thus they will speak the language with a foreign accent. Generally, the best predictor for successful acquisition of a language is early exposure. When it comes to sounds the child's perceptual system is most acute in the first year of life. Important neural circuitry is established during this period, and these connections lay the foundation for future language learning. Although some of the neural pathways that are laid within the first year of life may be reversible or established later in life, others are not. For languages, and especially for their sound systems, very early exposure is essential. The best strategy for optimizing your baby's linguistic abilities, then, is to expose her to languages as early as possible.

Baby's First Steps in Spanish makes it possible for you to do just that. By exposing babies to Spanish in their very first months of life, the CD provides children with their first steps in learning Spanish and other languages. If children's sound systems are maintained through continued exposure to Spanish, they will be better equipped with the necessary perceptual skills for learning Spanish and for speaking it without a foreign accent later in life. Moreover, they will be better prepared to learn subsequent languages and to reap the numerous cognitive, social, and academic benefits of multilingualism.

WHAT'S IN THIS PACKAGE

$\mathcal{T}$his package contains a compact disc (the CD) with a lyric sheet, and a book designed to guide you through your baby's first two years of language development.

The CD surrounds your baby with engaging Spanish sounds, phrases, and sentences. Children learn sounds best in combination with music and poetry, thus traditional Spanish children's songs and rhymes are included. The lyrics are specially designed to provide children with what they need for every stage of linguistic development from birth to age two. The entire inventory of Spanish sounds is presented throughout the CD, embedded in song and rhyme, and in the type of speech to which infants respond best: slow and melodic, with pure sounds. Structures they can grasp are repeated, and new information is added gradually.

The book tells you everything you need to know about how your baby develops her first and second languages from birth to age two. The first chapter, "Critical periods for birds and babies," explains why it is crucial for your baby to be exposed to a second language very early on in life. The second chapter, "Helping Your Baby Talk," gives advice, grounded in speech pathology and bilingualism research, on how to provide your child with an optimal environment for second-language learning, whether you speak the second language or not. For parents who are wondering how far to take this "multilingualism" concept, the third chapter, "Multilingualism: Is There Room for Two or More Languages in One Brain?" explains the educational benefits of multilingualism, such as improved cognition, literacy, and communication, and even some financial benefits it can bring to your child. This chapter also dispels common misconceptions about multilingualism. The fourth chapter, "Babies Learn to Talk: Steps in Language Development from Womb to Two," lays out in detail the milestones in your child's linguistic development—what your child is hearing and saying from her birth cry to her first miniature sentence. In the fifth chapter, "Making the Most of the CD," tips are provided on how to interact with your baby to help her best absorb the Spanish sounds on the CD. Because your ear for languages is not nearly as keen as your baby's, the sixth chapter, "The Sounds of Spanish," describes Spanish sounds so you can recognize and produce them. Finally, the "Resources for Parents" section provides a list of books and Web sites for parents interested in learning more about their baby's language development and about multilingualism in general.

We trust that you and your baby will take pleasure in your journey through the Spanish sounds and melodies. Language is a wonderful gift! You will soon be amazed at the remarkable linguistic feats your baby will perform as she playfully explores the world of a second language. *Baby's First Steps in Spanish* is here to open new worlds and new possibilities for both of you!

1. Critical Periods for Birds and Babies

> *"Young birds pass through an impressionable phase during which they are sensitive to exposure to song . . . The memory of song formed early in life—the 'acquired song template'—guides vocal development later in life."*
>
> —DANIEL MARGOLIASH IN "NEURAL PLASTICITY IN BIRDSONG LEARNING"

*I*f a baby bird is placed in isolation during its first few weeks of life, it may never learn its birdsong. Crowned sparrows that are not exposed to their species' song for their first seven weeks of life develop an abnormal song. Without a normal song, their bird life has hardships—they will be unable to maintain their territory or attract a mate. But let them hear even tape-recorded songs of their species during their first fifty days of life, and they will develop a normal, full-fledged sparrow song.

This time-bounded learning is not just for the birds. It is for your baby and for other little creatures as well. Windows of opportunity, called "critical periods," exist, during the time in which most animals are brilliant bundles of sensation, absorbing the world of light and sound, learning skills with ease and perfection. When these windows shut, they shut tightly and often irreversibly. Baby birds and humans become mere mortals, capable of learning some new skills but not others. Older children may learn new words in a language, for example, but they may never learn to trill an *r* like an Italian opera singer. If a skill has not been acquired before the critical period, learning it becomes difficult, and sometimes impossible.

As parents who want the best for your children, you need not worry. You will shower your babies with English sounds even before they are born (if that is the language you are speaking to them). The window of opportunity will not shut on their ability to learn English. Your children will absorb the sounds of your messages, along with their loving content, as they listen closely to the melody of English, the fascinating uneven rhythm, that funny *r* sound. Before you know it, your little birds will sing in impeccable English.

When it comes to learning a second or third language, your baby's first year of life is equally crucial. Babies are born poised and ready to learn any language in the world. For the first year of life, your child will have an uncanny ability to hear sounds in foreign languages with perfect clarity and precision, a skill he will all but lose by his first birthday. However, if he is surrounded continuously with sounds of foreign languages while his language window is open, he will have a head start on learning multiple languages, and on speaking them without a foreign accent.

IMPRINTING GULLIBLE GEESE

*W*hy do critical periods exist? In a classic experiment on the critical period for attachment formation in baby geese, the Austrian ethologist Konrad Lorenz became a parental figure to his unsuspecting subjects. Because Dr. Lorenz was the first moving being in the presence of newly-hatched geese, the baby geese took him irreversibly to be their parent, and swam behind him as if they were his progeny. When, on the other hand, the goslings' first exposure to Dr. Lorenz occurred a few days after hatching, it was too late—no such attachment was formed.

Nature planned this type of early "imprinting" for survival purposes. It is generally the case that the mother goose is present immediately after her babies hatch. The babies form an attachment with her and are, as a result, nourished and nurtured. It appears that the brain is "wired" in a way that permits animals to adapt to their environment. Genes supply the essential neural pathways, but experience triggers and fine-tunes the neural "wiring."

IMPRESSIONABLE HUMANS

$\mathcal{J}$ust as they are for other animals, critical periods are crucial to human development. The human brain has billions of neurons that can be connected in countless ways. The neural connections established in infancy and early childhood lay the foundation for future learning. Once these connections are established, only hard work can rewire them, and rewiring may not be entirely effective.

Of all human capacities, the one that most conspicuously relies on critical periods is language. Humans must hear a language early in life in order to master it. During critical periods, languages are learned easily and seamlessly. Children produce and combine sounds and words in their native language (or languages) even before they can walk on tiptoes—their rapid linguistic development is extraordinary and enviable. If you have tried learning a language after childhood, you know that the critical period is not forever—learning a language to perfection later in life is hard work, and rarely entirely successful.

SOUNDS: AN EARLY AND RIGID CURFEW

$\mathcal{B}$y what age must your child be exposed to a second language in order to speak it like a native speaker? As it turns out, the various components of language: sounds, grammar, and words, come with their own critical periods. The first and most rigid language curfew is imposed on speech sounds. Foreign accents are testaments to an early critical period for sounds; languages acquired beyond the early years of life will generally be spoken with an accent. Thus, for parents interested in exposing their young children to foreign languages, it is the sounds of the language that are of the greatest importance in your baby's first months and years.

INVENTORIES OF *OOHS* AND *AHS*

Just as a store keeps an inventory of its products, every language in the world has an inventory of speech sounds. In English, for example, we have fifteen vowel sounds and twenty-four consonant sounds. The consonants include a *p* sound, a *k* sound, an *l* sound, a *t* sound, an unusual *r* sound, and many more. The English vowel inventory has an *ee* sound, an *i* sound, and more vowel sounds than most languages of the world. In contrast, Spanish has twenty consonants, including a "rolled" *r* that sounds like a purr, and five vowels.

Spanish and Italian inventories contain fewer consonants and vowels than the English inventory. The Spanish trilled *r* sound is not found in English. This Spanish sound actually comes in a long and a short "version," and distinguishing the two is likely to present a particular challenge for an adult English speaker. The long *r* sound (represented by a double "r" in writing) is trilled or "rolled" for a few milliseconds longer than the short *r* sound. This small difference in pronunciation is used to distinguish words with entirely different meanings. So the word *perro* (with a long *r*) means "dog," whereas the word *pero* (with a short *r*) means "but." Similarly, Italian has words that are identical except for the length of their consonants. The word *sete* means "thirst," for example, whereas the word *sette* (with a long *t*) means "seven."

A BABY'S JOB DESCRIPTION

The first linguistic task your baby is presented with is identifying the inventory of sounds in the languages he hears. Newcomers to the United States marvel at their own children's rapid rate of learning flawless English. Within just a few years, young children learn to pronounce English like native speakers, while their parents may find themselves waging an uphill battle against those English sounds.

The secret of native-like pronunciation lies in the way children hear the sounds of speech. Decades of scientific research have provided overwhelming evidence that adults and infants hear the same sounds very differently. Perception, of course, sets the stage for production. When speakers do not have native-like perception of sounds in a language's inventory, they will speak that language with a foreign accent. From infant to toddler to adult, enormous changes take place in the perception of speech sounds.

WORLDLY BABIES

Infants are born with the ability to perceive all the possible sounds of the world's languages. For the first few months of life, they are citizens of the world. Infants in Paris, Florence, Buenos Aires, Tokyo, New York, Banjul, Prague, and Novosibirsk perceive any speech sound any language has to offer, and perceive it with extraordinary clarity. Even three- or four-day-old infants have been shown to distinguish sounds found across languages. That is, regardless of where they are born, infants can hear the difference between an *l* sound and an *r* sound. They hear the different sounds in the words *tu* "you" and *tout* "all" in French, in *perro* and *pero* in Spanish, and in *sette* and *sete* in Italian.

Sudden changes occur in the second half of babies' first year of life, forever altering their perceptual abilities. Infants are no longer able to distinguish several of the different sounds they distinctly heard just a few months before. By the age of seven months, for example, your baby may no longer hear the difference between *u* and *ü*—unless the sounds have been present continuously in his environment.

THE TIMING OF CHANGES

The timing of changes in perception differs from sound to sound. Six months is an important turning point for certain vowels, whereas

CRITICAL PERIODS FOR BIRDS AND BABIES

Do you hear what I hear?

Janet Werker and Richard Tees performed a classic experiment showing the changes in infant speech perception in the first year of life. They worked with two groups of subjects: babies in English-speaking households, and babies surrounded by Hindi. The researchers had the infants listen to two different *t* sounds that exist in Hindi. One of the *t* sounds is produced with the tongue touching the teeth, and the other is produced with the underside of the tongue touching the roof of the mouth. Six- to eight-month-old infants surrounded by Hindi or English had no trouble distinguishing these sounds. By ten to twelve months, however, infants surrounded by English could no longer tell the sounds apart, performing just like English-speaking adults. In contrast, infants of all ages surrounded by Hindi had no trouble at all discriminating the sounds.

the majority of changes in your baby's perception will take place in the second half of his first year of life. Of course, exceptions do exist and people may be able to "reverse" their perceptual changes if they are exposed continuously to a second language well before puberty. But training in adulthood is typically far less successful than language learning in childhood.

WHY DO WE STOP HEARING FOREIGN SOUNDS SO WELL?

Why can't we be citizens of the world forever? Unlike in French, in which *tu* means "you" and *tout* means "all," in English, the sounds *u* and *ü* do not distinguish words—*ü* does not even exist. Similarly, in Japanese, *l* and *r* do not distinguish words—there is only one sound somewhere between *l* and *r*. If we are not exposed to a language, what is the use of being able to distinguish all of its unique nuances? As infants' skills in foreign languages decline, they turn their expertise to the languages in their surroundings. Your baby is paying attention to aspects of speech that will help him distinguish words in English and other languages he might actually hear.

FAST FORWARD TO ADULTHOOD: WHY ACCENTS HAPPEN

We now fast forward to adulthood. Why do adults learning a foreign language have difficulty pronouncing some of the new sounds? The answer lies primarily in perception: they do not hear the sounds the way a native speaker hears them. Consequently, they will not produce the sounds like a native speaker.

Listeners integrate sounds they hear in foreign languages into their own inventory, matching them as closely as possible with their native language sounds. When English-speaking adults hear the French vowel sound *ü* (produced with the tongue in *ee* position and the lips pursed) in *tu*, they may *perceive* it as *oo*. This is because *oo*, a sound that does exist in the English inventory (as in *coo*), seems closest to the French vowel in *tu*. As a result, they might *produce* the sound *oo* for both French vowels in *vue* "view" or *vous* "you"— and be judged to have a foreign accent. Similarly, English speakers tend not to pay much attention to the extended *t* and *r* sounds in Italian *sette* "seven" and Spanish *perro* "dog" because these sounds do not exist in English. They tend to hear and pronounce the sounds as regular short consonants because they no longer perceive sounds the way they did as infants. Now they hear them through the filter of English. As a result, they have a foreign accent.

Unfortunately, misperceiving or misarticulating these "nuances" can lead to trouble. Just as English has a similar-sounding but vulgar counterpart to words such as *beach*, so do words such as *coup* "blow" in French or

Italian *anno* "year." Generally, though, native speakers are more likely to be amused than offended.

DON'T ACCENTS JUST COME FROM LACK OF PRACTICE?

In the past, it has been argued that accents, rather than being caused by misperception, result from poor attitudes, bad habits, or difficulties with sensorimotor pathways for pronunciation. A common argument against "accented perception" as a cause of accented production comes from people who feel that they hear sounds just like a native speaker, but that they just have difficulty coordinating their muscles to produce the sound.

Research indicates that this is not the case. It is true that muscles must sometimes be trained to produce particular sounds, and some gestures are muscularly more complicated than others. Some people who lisp, for example, can hear the difference between *s* and *th* sounds, but have trouble creating an *s*-like sound without placing their tongue

between their teeth. But for foreign accents (as for many articulation disorders), perception is still considered the primary culprit, even for speakers who feel they hear and sometimes produce the sounds impeccably. If a person does not consistently produce a sound accurately, he is not perceiving the sound as clearly as a native speaker does. Some English speakers may hear that there is a difference between Spanish *pero* and *perro*, for example, and produce it accurately on occasion. But increase the anxiety level just a tad, and the English speaker will no longer be able to hear the difference, whereas even a nervous Spanish speaker at a noisy restaurant will still not have any trouble. The English speaker does not have as stable a mental representation of the sound as the Spanish speaker does, and this leads to inconsistent production.

EVEN PASSIVE EXPOSURE TO SOUNDS LEAVES ITS MARK

Studies show that even when there is no rem-

One of these sounds is not like the other: How we know what infants perceive

"High amplitude sucking" is one method typically used to determine infants' ability to perceive different sounds. The children suck on a non-nutritive nipple and a regular or "baseline" sucking rate is determined. A sound, such as *bu*, is then presented. The sound is repeated every time the infants suck the nipple, and soon babies discover that they control exactly when they hear the sound. They will listen to *bu, bu, bu, bu*, gently sucking on the nipple. After listening to the same sound, they may become a little bored, a little sleepy, and suck slowly.

Suddenly, the new stimulus, *bü*, is presented. Six-month-old infants living in any country will perk up and suck the nipple more vigorously, intrigued by this new sound. The more intense sucking signals to the researcher that the child has perceived the sound *bü* as different from *bu*. The researchers conclude (as did professors Linda Polka and Janet Werker) that the six-month-old is therefore sensitive to the difference between the sounds *u* and *ü*. If the infant has not heard the difference between the first set of *bu* stimuli and the second set (*bü*), as is the case for many ten-month-olds in the United States (but not in Germany), he will continue to suck at the slow, sleepy baseline rate he sucked on for *bu*.

nant of vocabulary or grammar in the language, the sound system of the language may persist. This is true even if contact with a particular language was passive and short-lived. The researchers we have already encountered, Richard Tees and Janet Werker, in further work on Hindi *t*'s, studied subjects living in North America who were exposed to

CRITICAL PERIODS FOR BIRDS AND BABIES

Hindi for only their first year or two of life and had no further exposure to it. In adulthood, when they were tested on the Hindi contrast, their perceptual abilities were far superior to those of most native English listeners, even those with training in Hindi. We conclude that even passive exposure within the first two years of life may have a permanent impact on individuals' perceptual skills.

Similarly, the author of this book is still capable of producing a sound considered one of the most difficult in the world: the Czech ř (r háček), even though she barely speaks a word of the language any more. This is simply the result of having lived in Prague as a young child. Interestingly, when she worked as pronunciation coach for the talented puppeteers behind the voices of *Sesame Street's* characters, she was unable to convince Big Bird or Elmo that the r in the name *Jiří*, the Czech equivalent of "George," was different from the r in the word *rybíz* "currant"—they simply could not hear the difference. This is not surprising, considering what we know about neur-

al connections solidifying in early childhood.

....

SOUND CONCLUSION

....

Although the precise mechanism for how changes in perception occur is not known, there is no question that these changes do occur and that they occur primarily within a baby's first year. It is not understood why some people can learn a second language starting at age five, or even ten, and speak it with virtually no accent. What is known, however, is that children surrounded by one, two, or more languages continuously from infancy will typically speak those languages without a trace of a foreign accent. This is precisely why we have designed the attached CD to surround infants with Spanish sounds during their all-important early years.

CRITICAL PERIOD FOR LEARNING THE GRAMMAR OF A SECOND LANGUAGE

*F*or learning the grammar of a second language, the timetable may not be quite as tight as for learning sounds: Skills dwindle over time, but most dramatically in late childhood. Jacqueline Johnson and Elissa Newport studied native speakers of Chinese and Korean who had immigrated to the United States between ages three and thirty-nine. The older the immigrants were when they arrived in the United States (after early childhood), the lower their scores were on a grammatical test of English, with a bit of a plunge occurring at puberty. Neurological data are in line with these findings. In a brain-imaging study, Karl Kim and his colleagues found that the languages in bilinguals who had been exposed to two languages from birth were stored "closer together" in the frontal lobe of their brains than in bilinguals who had learned their second language at an average age of eleven.

Thus, just as for the perception of sounds, researchers overwhelmingly agree that the earlier a child is exposed to a second language on a consistent basis, the more native-like his knowledge of the language will be. Vocabulary can be learned successfully throughout a person's lifetime, but the grammar and sounds of languages cannot.

CONCLUSION: DON'T DILLY-DALLY

$\mathcal{I}$t is wonderful that you are weighing all of your baby's options for learning a second language—but the evidence suggests you oughtn't delay. The first year of life stocks your baby with sounds for his inventory. Grammar comes a little later, but it is also best learned in early childhood. Perhaps your child will be one of the chosen few who can learn language past the critical period. But remember: These are the exceptions rather than the rule. For the rest of the world, early exposure is crucial.

2. Helping Your Baby Talk

IN THIS CHAPTER YOU WILL DISCOVER HOW TO HELP YOUR BABY SPEAK ANY NUMBER OF LANGUAGES BY . . .

★ SURROUNDING YOUR BABY WITH A LANGUAGE OR LANGUAGES

★ SPEAKING "PARENTESE"

★ REPEATING, REWARDING, AND EXPANDING YOUR BABY'S BABBLINGS

★ NEVER PUNISHING YOUR CHILD'S ERRORS

★ READING ALOUD TO YOUR BABY

★ DELIGHTING IN LANGUAGE

★ LOOKING OUT FOR LANGUAGE DELAYS AND MIDDLE-EAR INFECTIONS

A most important factor in raising a bilingual child is the language that surrounds language [. . .]. Language growth in children requires the minimum of pruning—these are tender, young plants. Correcting language continuously, getting the child to repeat sentences, is the kind of pruning that research shows to have almost no effect, even a negative effect on language growth. The role of the language gardener is to provide a stimulating soil—a variety of pleasurable environments for language growth.

—COLIN BAKER IN *A PARENTS' AND TEACHERS' GUIDE TO BILINGUALISM*

*B*abies all over the world say their first word near their first birthday, whether they are learning one language or more. Universally, they cry, they coo, they babble, they talk, all in the same order and at roughly the same ages. In the previous chapter, we witnessed nature steering babies away from hearing all of the possible sounds of the world's languages and helping them zero in on the sounds around them. Clearly, nature exerts a powerful force on babies' learning.

So what does this mean for nurture? Should you sit back in silence and watch your child's language unfold? Absolutely not! Sparrows must hear their sparrow song. Your babies must hear your language or languages—and they must have good reason to speak. As loving and caring parents, you want to know what you can do to help your baby talk in one language or more. Whether or not you speak a foreign language yourself, you have questions about how your baby best learns the language or languages in her sur-roundings. The following is advice typically given by speech pathologists, linguists, and experts on bilingualism.

WHAT'S NURTURE GOT TO DO WITH IT?

*B*ecause your baby is, to some degree, "pre-wired" for language, you cannot shoulder the entire responsibility for her linguistic development. No matter what you do, you will not be able to train your six-month-old to babble, "Ooh là là" or your two-year-old to recite Hamlet's soliloquy. But you can provide a loving and enriching environment in which your baby will want to communicate, a setting in which languages will thrive.

CHEERFUL EARFULS: SURROUNDING YOUR CHILD WITH LANGUAGE

One of the biggest favors you can do for your child is to surround her with language, to be pleasantly talkative. If you are exposing your child to two languages, she has two systems to learn, thus double the task monolinguals are faced with. Speak two languages to your baby if you can, or better yet, speak one language and have your spouse speak the other. If you do not speak a second language, you can still shower your baby with an abundance of foreign sounds by tuning your radio to a foreign language station, playing the attached CD, or investing in other foreign language audio products. (Many are available through the Internet sites listed in the "Resources" section.) Children do not learn language merely by imitating what they hear. They pay attention to sounds, extract patterns, associate words with objects, and notice the different ways language can be used. The more language your child hears, the more material she will have to work with.

Some of us are already good at talking to ourselves, others are not. If you are not a chatty person by nature, you can train yourself to chat (in English or other languages) as you go about your daily tasks. Your child is soaking up more than she lets on: the sounds, the words, the meanings. While you feed your baby, for example, name the various foods.

Say "Drink" when she drinks, "Open" when something is opened, and ask "More?" You are, by far, her most important linguistic role model. Unbeknownst to your child, she is learning nouns, verbs, and adjectives! But remember to keep the "lessons" light and pleasurable for both of you. Enthusiasm will engage your child—sermons will not.

ICING ON THE CAKE:
REPEAT, REWARD, AND EXPAND

Yet another technique for helping babies talk is done instinctively by most parents. But by becoming aware of what you are doing, you can make the most of the strategy. When you speak to your baby, you will often repeat what she says, and add a little more. For example, your child might point to a dog and say, "Doggie." You might say, "Yes, doggie. Nice doggie." She might repeat, "Nice doggie." You have reinforced your child's utterance through repetition, and shown her how to add a word to the phrase. The attached CD uses the concept of repeating, rewarding, and expanding,

"Parentese": Doing what comes naturally

Intuitively, you are probably doing much of what speech pathologists recommend. Without enrolling in language classes, you are probably speaking "motherese," henceforth called "parentese," to your children. This is a special style of speech heard all over the world when parents speak to their children. You might say "My sweeeet baaabyyy," the melody rising and falling, hitting notes you did not know you could reach. The vowels are pure—they stretch out and linger. You spread your lips, then pucker. As silly as you might feel, you are doing just what the doctor ordered! Using melodic intonation and repetition, you are emphasizing those sounds your child is particularly open to absorbing. Your child has less difficulty processing slow speech, exaggerated tone, and drawn-out vowels than normal speech. So use that baby talk in any language with abandon! All of it is linguistic and all of it is communication. The sounds on the *Baby's First Steps* CD contain "parentese" in Spanish to complement your efforts.

with appropriate Spanish structures for your child's particular stage of development.

Putting words together to form phrases does not come automatically to children. The way phrases are constructed differs from language to language, so children need to learn how it is done in their particular language. Soon your baby will be spontaneously saying

"nice doggie" and "black doggie," and eventually "nice black doggie." Through this type of conversation, your child will learn how to add complexity to her sentences. It should be noted that if your child is raised bilingually, she will not only learn two words for the same items, but she will also learn to combine words in different ways. In French, Spanish,

19

and Italian, for example, the adjective will usually follow the noun instead of preceding it (*e.g.*, Spanish *el perro negro,* literally, "the dog black").

To use this technique most efficiently, it will be helpful for you to determine the linguistic stage your child has reached, which you can do by referring to the "Babies Learn to Talk" chapter. With the help of the section on steps in language development, you will learn whether your child is at the babbling, one-word, or mini-sentence stage of production, for instance. Your task is to match your baby's level of development, but also to go a little beyond it. So if she is babbling repetitive syllables (for example, "nanana"), you might babble back, but also use jargon (for example, "nanana ninonu"). As she begins to produce single words (using our example of "doggie"), you might say "Doggie. Nice doggie." When she begins to combine words, you might do the same and also say short sentences. You are rewarding her sweet speech and putting icing on the cake.

Interactions with your little one should be conversations rather than monologues. Your child speaks when she has something to communicate, whether it be hunger, sadness, love, or a brand new discovery. She may use sounds she has never heard or gestures you do not quite understand. But she wants to be heard and appreciated.

Good listening encourages good talking. An important and enjoyable task you have ahead of you is carrying on real conversations in any language with your child, regardless of the complexity of her speech. Speak directly, clearly, and slowly, using short phrases for easier processing. If you say, "Cozy?" and she says, "Goo!!" and you tuck her in a little more, you have had a terrific conversation. She will listen to what you have to say and sometimes wait to respond. You can do the same. Not only are you communicating, but you are also practicing turn-taking, a basic of adult-like conversation.

WHY CORRECTION AND PUNISHMENT DO NOT WORK

Noam Chomsky, the Freud of linguistics, noted that children do not learn language through being corrected: Parents can correct them all they want, but children will not learn until they have independently figured out how language works. Moreover, until children understand what language is (usually in the toddler years), they have no idea what parents are doing when they are correcting their language. For example, if a child says "doo" for *juice* while reaching for the juice, and the parent says "No, it's not *doo*. I won't give you the juice until you use the right word. Say *juice* instead," the child will become perplexed, distraught, and very thirsty. A much more gentle and effective method is for you to lovingly respond, "Juice? You want juice!" as you hand your baby a cup of juice. This is modeling, not correcting, and it is highly instructive. Your child will learn to associate the word *juice* with what she has been drinking, and eventually understand the words *you* and *want*.

What parents must not do is punish their children for "incorrect" utterances. Parents have been known to pretend they do not understand their child or force their children to say a word correctly. Children who are punished for their errors will become self-conscious, ashamed, and quiet. This is not only unfortunate, but it is also counterproductive. The magic of children's rapid linguistic development has much do with their uninhibited chattiness, their lack of concern about making blatant errors, and their joyful desire to communicate.

If you are raising your child bilingually, she might occasionally mix up words in various languages. This is a harmless and temporary side effect of learning two languages at once—and certainly nothing to be punished. This behavior will, in all likelihood, resolve itself with continued exposure to both languages.

WATCH ME READ: THE IMPORTANCE OF PRE-LITERACY

In recent years, a focus of preschool education has been pre-literacy skills. You, too, can prepare your child to learn to read and write by giving her an early understanding of the importance of such skills in all of the languages she is hearing. Reading wonderful and magical books aloud will awaken any child's interest in the written word, particularly if you point to the writing in books as you read. You might also show your child your shopping lists, point to street signs, give her crayons, and encourage any scribbles she might produce. If you don't speak a second language, you can still point to pictures and writing in books when your baby is hearing sounds in foreign languages. (For example, as you listen to the Spanish sounds on the *Baby's First Steps* CD, you might point to the lyrics on the accompanying lyrics sheet.) Your child is learning an important association between sound and print. Joy and an abundance of colors will provide your baby with early information and positive messages about reading, writing, and language in general.

DELIGHTING IN LANGUAGES

Above all, it is important for you to delight in languages, delight in the banter, delight in puns, delight in the sounds on the CD, delight in your child's magical touch with sounds. Conversations that are loving and rewarding work far better than anxiety-ridden sermons on how your baby should speak. Every error she makes is a step forward in her development. When she makes silly sounds, such as explosive noises or screaming, she is exploring her voice and her ability to create and match sounds, sometimes in multiple languages. Playful exploration is the key to successful language development and to the all-important bond between you and your child. *Baby's First Steps* lets children play with the Spanish language early, while they are at their peak of linguistic brilliance and unabashed whimsy.

In order to make learning two languages

enjoyable and desirable for your child, it is important that you not reveal anxiety about surrounding her with more than one language. If you are not comfortable with your child's learning a foreign language, she may become uncomfortable and unmotivated. Becoming more informed about bilingualism by reading the "Multilingualism" chapter, referring to the "Resources" section, or consulting with other parents and professionals will help you resolve some questions and relieve some anxiety. If you are eager to give your child two languages and rejoice in her remarkable linguistic feats, she will take pleasure in developing both languages.

IF PROBLEMS ARISE

IT'S "YES," NOT "SÍ": WHAT TO DO IF YOUR CHILD REJECTS A SECOND LANGUAGE

When they reach later childhood, some children will rebel and refuse to speak or listen to a second language. Perhaps the "cool people" speak one language and not the other. Whatever the reason, if your child refuses to speak a particular language, you cannot force her. Remember—you are the gardener. Your job is pruning, not legislating. You can only discuss the issue and hear each other out. Perhaps it will comfort you to know that, regardless of the outcome, you have already helped your child gain many of the benefits that come with having been exposed to multiple languages early in life.

SPEECH AND LANGUAGE DELAYS AND DISORDERS

The causes of language delays are diverse and often unknown. They include prenatal or natal complications, physical delays, emotional disturbances, extreme paucity of input from parents, and chronic middle-ear infections. When bilingual children have language delays or disorders (such as stuttering), well-meaning teachers and clinicians who are not knowledgeable about bilingual issues may turn to bilingualism as the culprit.

23

"What, mommy?": Chronic ear infections

A correlation exists between children who have speech disorders and those who had chronic middle-ear infections in their first year of life. It appears that these children's ears were blocked during the critical period when sounds are most easily learned, and as a result, they did not learn to master the sound system of their languages while their brain was at its most receptive. If children have been raised bilingually, the effects of ear infections are found in both languages. It is important for you to remain abreast of your child's hearing status; hearing screenings may alert you to possible deficits.

Bilingualism does not cause language delays or disorders. Countries in which people are bilingual or even trilingual do not have a higher incidence of language delays or disorders than other countries. What matters much more than how many languages parents speak to their child is how they actually speak to a child. If you follow the suggestions above, for effective and encouraging linguistic immersion, you are creating "stimulating soil," the best possible environment for language growth.

If you do find that your child is not progressing normally through her linguistic development (see the "Babies Learn to Talk" chapter), it is important that you contact a qualified speech pathologist who has knowledge of and experience with bilingual issues. This should be done in a timely manner—as we know, time constraints do exist for language learning. But don't panic. Some children need a long time to absorb language before they begin to show results. Einstein was one such child, and his parents did consult a doctor—he was no less than three when he began to speak.

3. Multilingualism: Is There Room for Two or More Languages in One Brain?

IN THIS CHAPTER, YOU WILL WEIGH THE PROS AND CONS OF MULTILIN-
GUALISM BY LEARNING ABOUT ITS BENEFITS . . .

★ INCREASED COGNITIVE FLEXIBILITY
★ POSITIVE EFFECTS ON LITERACY AND ACADEMIC PERFORMANCE
★ INCREASED AWARENESS OF LANGUAGE
★ FACILITY WITH LEARNING A THIRD LANGUAGE
★ BROADENING OF SOCIAL, ECONOMIC, AND CULTURAL HORIZONS
★ PLEASURE AND SATISFACTION IN KNOWING MULTIPLE LANGUAGES

AND ITS INCONVENIENCES . . .

★ TEMPORARY WORD SUBSTITUTIONS AND SPELLING ERRORS
★ SLIGHTLY SLOWER PROCESSING OF A SECOND LANGUAGE IN NAMING TASKS
★ FEELING PRESSURE TO ACT AS A TRANSLATOR

"It [bilingualism] broadens your scope. It means you have two worlds instead of one (friends, cultural aspects, job possibilities)."

—FRANÇOIS GROSJEAN IN *LIFE WITH TWO LANGUAGES*

*N*ow you are conversing with your brand new baby in all the right ways, showering him with English and Spanish sounds. Perhaps you, your spouse, and your nanny speak three different languages, and you have great multilingual aspirations for your child. Or perhaps the Spanish on the CD is the only foreign presence at home and you have not yet determined how much foreign language immersion you want for your baby. Regardless of your state of bilingualism, this chapter will help you decide what is best for your child by demystifying several notions attached to multilingualism and exploring the advantages and disadvantages of learning more than one language.[2]

MIXED MESSAGES

*P*arents of bilinguals face mixed messages and strong opinions about their choice to raise children bilingually. Traditionally, a fear exists in largely monolingual countries such as the United States that learning a second language will do damage to a child's first language or to other capacities. Older books on child rearing have even warned parents that teaching a child two names for an item will result in linguistic and mental deficits, and teachers have been known to point to bilingualism as the cause of children's linguistic, cognitive, academic, and social difficulties.

Colin Baker, an expert on bilingualism, points out that a good number of authors of child-care books are medical writers who may know a great deal about certain aspects of a child's development, but are not exactly versed in research on linguistics, bilingualism, or bilingual child development. It is easy to make bilingualism a culprit, but there is a paucity of evidence to back up any such claims.[3]

---

[2]The terms *bilingualism* and *multilingualism* will be used interchangeably to denote knowing two or more languages.

[3]Research-based sources are listed in the "Resources for Parents" section to become better versed in the facts about bilingual language acquisition and related topics. Colin Baker's *A Parents' and*

RESEARCH FINDINGS ON MULTILINGUALISM

$\mathcal{D}$ecades of research have found that, for the most part, the opposite is true: Multilinguals perform at least as well as, and often better than, monolingual children when it comes to languages, school, and social and professional life. In reality, for the overwhelming majority of the world's population, lifelong multilingualism is the norm rather than the exception. Fear of multilingualism appears to be an American neurosis. Despite this country's ethnic and linguistic diversity few elementary schools in the United States offer foreign languages. Knowing what we know now about critical periods in language development, it follows that the majority of native English-speaking Americans never become proficient in a foreign language. In most countries of the world, people speak several languages proficiently and without resulting complications.

The following are two pertinent conclusions that have been drawn from the converging strands of research in areas such as linguistics, bilingualism, and second language acquisition: First, learning a second language does not interfere with the development of a first language. Second, multilingualism does affect linguistic, academic, social, and cognitive development; the overwhelming majority of these effects are positive. Both of these conclusions will be addressed.

ROOM FOR ONE MORE?

Parents wonder if their baby's little brain has room for another language. The answer is, unequivocally, that there is plenty of room for

---

Teachers' Guide to Bilingualism is particularly recommended, as it is a research-based book designed for parents. It does justice to topics such as reading, writing, and bilingual education, which are beyond the scope of this book.

27

The many faces of multilingualism

Multilingualism comes in all varieties. Monique, a French mother of two young bilingual children, was raised bilingually herself and speaks absolutely fluent French and English. But as a child she made odd comments in English, such as, "Alas, that foolish maiden," when a pedestrian walked in front of a taxi (a result of listening to fairy tales in English early in life). As an adult, when she speaks English, she calls corn flakes "petals" and says the French "euh" instead of the English "um" when she hesitates. She also speaks proficient German and can get by in Polish.

Monique's daughters, living in France, hear English primarily from their mother and French from everyone else. At age four, Lisa pointed to the doghouse and said "chien maison," a direct translation of the English compound word (literally "dog house"), when the French word is actually *niche*. Now Lisa insists on speaking English with English speakers, whereas her younger sister Mélina answers in French when a question is posed in English. Their father, Joël, speaks French, but learned English in adulthood and speaks it with a characteristic French accent. All of these individuals are bilingual.

multiple languages, and that, in most of the world, little and big brains are successfully filled with at least two languages.

When it comes to building a vocabulary, children surrounded by two languages have twice as many words to learn as do monolinguals. Studies have found that bilingual children have smaller vocabularies in each language than do their monolingual counterparts. However, if their total vocabulary is taken into consideration (the number of words in both languages combined), their vocabulary

The bilingual lexicon

Large bodies of literature have been written about how the "bilingual lexicon" (a bilingual's mental dictionary) might work. Researchers generally believe that bilinguals have one conceptual system, not two. Concepts are thought to be connected to, but largely independent of, any particular language. The difference between a monolingual and a bilingual is that the monolingual will have one word for an object, whereas a bilingual will have two words for it (e.g., *foot* and *pied*). This model gives us no reason to believe that a conceptual system would become burdened by a second language.

is far larger than that of monolinguals.

IS LANGUAGE DEVELOPMENT SLOWER IN TWO LANGUAGES THAN IN ONE?

Parents often wonder whether learning two languages slows the development of any particular language. The answer is that bilingualism is unlikely to slow language learning. Monolingual and bilingual learners progress through the same stages of acquisition in the same order (described in the "Babies Learn to Talk" chapter). Most studies agree that they progress at the same rate, although some authors (such as a writer of child development books, Penelope Leach) claim that bilinguals' early language development may be slightly slower, but that they soon catch up. Like monolinguals, bilinguals learn their first words at approximately one year, two- to four-word combinations during the second year, and longer sentences thereafter.

Naturally, variation and individual differences are the rule in all areas of child development. If you are concerned that your child

> ## Testing language awareness
>
> A test of linguistic awareness was performed by psychology professor Ellen Bialystok. Children were asked to identify the word that was bigger, in pairs such as *caterpillar* and *skunk*. Bilinguals were better able to answer the question correctly, keeping word size and meaning apart, whereas monolinguals were more likely to answer according to the size of the animal rather than the size of the word. Once your infant has become a young child, you could ask her similar questions to determine whether she has grasped the concept of language.

might be delayed—that is, by more than a few months—you are advised to consult a qualified speech pathologist (see the section on "Speech and language delays and disorders" in the previous chapter).

LEARNING A SECOND LANGUAGE HELPS THE FIRST LANGUAGE

Bilinguals have an acute awareness of language that is unmatched by their monolingual peers. By the age of two, bilinguals can usually point to familiar speakers and identify which language they speak, a task that would baffle most monolinguals of the same age. Monolinguals generally have relative difficulty separating the names of items from the items themselves, that is, separating sound and meaning. Bilinguals, in contrast, have a strong sense of the *arbitrariness* of words—that words are just labels attached to things.

ADVANTAGES FOR READING AND WRITING

Why should awareness of language matter? Linguistic awareness has been found to correlate highly with academic success, particularly with reading and writing. Bilinguals tend to learn to read faster than monolinguals. Reading depends upon knowing the structure of language, and also recognizing that language is actually a set of arbitrary labels or symbols. Bilinguals know that two symbols exist for every word. Written languages are just a third set of symbols. Bilinguals have already grasped the notion of arbitrary labels, and they transfer this idea quickly to writing.

ADVANTAGE FOR LEARNING YET ANOTHER LANGUAGE

An important advantage to linguistic awareness in two languages is that it helps people learn a third language. Because they know that two systems exist for expressing the same thought, it is not a leap to think that a third system might do the same. For example, an English/Spanish bilingual understands that words may have gender. That is, whereas English has just the article *the,* Spanish has both *el* and *la*. Words with the article *el* are masculine, even if they stand for things (e.g.,

el vino "the wine"), and words with the article *la* are feminine (e.g., *la mesa* "the table"). Thus, it is easier for an English/Spanish bilingual to learn French, Italian, or Russian, for example, which have gender, than for an English monolingual, who would first have to become used to the concept that words for objects can be masculine or feminine.

Another important linguistic domain that carries over to a third language is sound. Knowing two languages increases the sound inventory available to bilinguals. Thus a French/English bilingual already knows the sound *ü* (as in *vue* "view") and will have little trouble acquiring the German *ü* sound (as in *Bücher* "books"). Moreover, vocabulary carries over from language to language. A Spanish/English bilingual will have less difficulty learning French than will an English monolingual, because French and Spanish have similar vocabularies (for example, *number* is *numéro* in French and *número* in Spanish).

Language affects our senses

Mbahasa Melayu, a Malaysian language, has different words signifying several degrees of saltiness (for example, as salty as soy sauce, as salty as sea water, as salty as salt, and horribly salty). Speakers of this language can make finer distinctions about how much salt is in a solution than can English speakers tasting the same solution. Thus an extra language may actually influence our senses in subtle ways, causing us to experience the world a little more discerningly.

NEGATIVE EFFECTS ON LANGUAGE

The benefits of multilingualism do not come without their inconveniences. For some linguistic tasks, processing in a second language might take slightly longer than in the native language. For example, native German speakers who have lived in Sweden for more than seventeen years (and are fluent in both languages) are .2 seconds slower at naming objects in Swedish than are Swedish monolinguals. But most would argue that speaking a second language, even if one can't speak it quite as quickly as a native speaker, is still more satisfying than not speaking a second language at all.

Knowing two languages does sometimes cause temporary word and spelling substitutions, but these glitches are usually recognized and corrected quickly. Children may confuse spelling in one language with the spelling in another language as they learn to read and write or unintentionally use words from a different language while speaking.

Furthermore, temporary misconceptions might occur in bilingual children. For exam ple, the author spoke French to her mother and English to her father. She therefore assumed, for a while, that all women spoke French and all men spoke English and consequently greeted women in French and men in English! But like most challenges that arise for bilinguals, this misconception was soon resolved.

TWICE AS SMART?
POSITIVE EFFECTS ON COGNITION

Superior flexibility and creativity in problem-solving have consistently been found in studies of bilinguals. For example, if given a tool or an object, bilinguals can think of far more numerous and creative ways to use it than can monolinguals.

HOW DO BILINGUALS FEEL ABOUT THEIR BILINGUALISM?

*I*n his book *Life with Two Languages*, François Grosjean reported what bilinguals liked most and what they found most inconvenient about their bilingualism.

PROS OF BILINGUALISM

Bilinguals described the following advantages: Having two worlds rather than one . . . feeling at home wherever they are . . . communicating with different people all over the world . . . traveling with more ease . . . being able to penetrate communities better . . . having open-mindedness bred by communication with people from different cultures . . . having the ability to read literature in its original language . . . having more job opportunities.

A benefit not mentioned by these bilinguals is having a sense of accomplishment and self-esteem, particularly for individuals who put great effort into learning languages in adulthood. Moreover, new languages bring with them new perspectives on old concepts. Languages are free travel: They challenge the obvious and propose the unexpected. Treats in language learning include clever words, such as the German word *Handschuh* (literally, "hand-shoe"), meaning "glove," and the Russian word for "pillow,"

Famous bilinguals

Marlene Dietrich	Albert Einstein	Vladimir Nabokov	Frédéric Chopin
Joseph Conrad	Sophia Loren	Noam Chomsky	Sigmund Freud

podushka, which translates literally as "under the ear."

CONS OF BILINGUALISM

Grosjean's informants found the following inconveniences of being bilingual: Being forced to act as a translator . . . mixing up words from different languages within a sentence . . . needing adjustment in childhood . . . having difficulty discussing certain topics in one of the languages . . . and dealing with biculturalism.

Multilinguals generally had positive feelings about knowing multiple languages, and several could not even think of any inconveniences.

WILL THIS CD MAKE YOUR CHILD BILINGUAL?

*P*erhaps you have weighed the pros and cons of bilingualism and concluded that it is virtually harmless and significantly beneficial. Will the attached CD make your baby bilingual? Of course, it cannot in itself turn your baby into a bilingual. But it is a first step paving the way toward bilingualism if you choose this route. Your child needs active interaction in a language over several years in order to become proficient in Spanish or any other language.

Suggestions are provided (in "Making the Most of the CD") for making the CD as effective as possible for your child's linguistic development. Because your baby is so acutely aware of sounds, he will pay close attention to the Spanish inventory of sounds and continue to learn the sounds, words, and concepts until his second year of life. The more your child is actively involved with a language, the more fully he is likely to learn it. If you are eager to have him become a balanced bilingual, you may consider having a Spanish caretaker or sending him to a Spanish-speaking play group and a Spanish-speaking school.

WHAT IF YOU WANT THE CD AND NOTHING ELSE?

$\mathcal{E}$ ven if you have no plans to immerse your child in two languages in the future, exposing your child to the Spanish sounds on the CD is still helpful, and certainly not harmful. We learned this powerfully from the experiment on Hindi sounds described in the "Critical Periods for Birds and Babies" chapter. Even limited experience in a second language may leave an indelible mark.

HAVING WEIGHED THE PROS AND CONS

$\mathcal{W}$ hat does all this mean for your child? If you raise your child bilingually, minor glitches may occur, but these usually resolve themselves quickly enough to allow your child to reap the linguistic, cognitive, social, academic, and personal benefits of multilingualism.

4. Babies Learn to Talk: Steps in Language Development from Womb to Two

IN THIS CHAPTER, YOU WILL DISCOVER THAT YOUR BABY CAN HEAR . . .

★ THE RHYTHM OF YOUR SPEECH EVEN BEFORE SHE IS BORN

★ ALL OF THE SOUNDS OF THE LANGUAGES SURROUNDING HER

★ YOUR CLEAR, SLOW, MELODIC "PARENTESE"

★ WORDS, WORDS, AND MORE WORDS

AND THAT YOUR BABY CAN SAY . . .

★ ALL SORTS OF SOUNDS AS SHE EXPLORES HER VOCAL TRACT

★ BABBLINGS IN THE LANGUAGES SHE HEARS

★ "JARGON" USING THE SOUNDS AND RHYTHMS SHE HEARS

★ HER FIRST TRUE WORDS, SPECIFIC TO HER LANGUAGE AND CULTURE

★ TELEGRAPHIC SPEECH, USING PERFECT WORD ORDER

Anyone who has ever responded to the cries of a howling infant may find it difficult to believe the etymology of the word infant. The source of our word is the Latin word infans . . . meaning "a little child; strictly, one who does not yet speak."

—*THE AMERICAN HERITAGE DICTIONARY*, THIRD EDITION

*E*vidently, the ancient Romans did not know what we know now: Little babies do talk, absorb speech, and communicate, sometimes even better than adults! We also know that before they are born, babies listen closely to the sounds they hear through the uterine walls. When they emerge at birth, they are already drawn to their mother's voice and to the language they will be learning.

What exactly is your baby hearing? Why is she babbling? This chapter will guide you through what your child is experiencing in the worlds of language and communication. As we have noted, babies vary tremendously in their progression through the stages of language development. Some will take small steps, and others will take steps backward before moving ahead. Yet others will leap ahead, skipping several steps.

Your baby will pace herself appropriately, alloting time and energy to master other important tasks, such as sitting, standing, walking, feeding herself, toilet training, and putting on her shoes.

THE FIRST SIX MONTHS

WHAT YOUR BABY IS HEARING
FROM BIRTH TO SIX MONTHS

I got rhythm

Through the uterine wall, babies hear the rhythm of their mothers speech. Even four-day-old infants show preference for their mother's voice and for female voices in general. Newborns recognize their mother tongue as different from other languages and prefer to listen to it.

Speech sounds of the world

The first few months of life are the time when infants perceive all of the possible sounds in world languages. They are keenly aware of the differences among all of the French nasal sounds, they hear the rolling *r*'s in Italian and Spanish, the different tones in Thai, the differ-

37

BABIES' STEPS IN LANGUAGE DEVELOPMENT

AGE	LANGUAGE BABIES PERCEIVE	LANGUAGE BABIES PRODUCE
Birth– 6 months	• Rhythms in any language of the world • Vowels and consonants in any language of the world • Familiar voices	• The birth cry and other reflexive sounds • Cooing, gurgling, and laughing • Vocal experiments: screaming, putting lips together, and blowing
6–12 months	• Fewer and fewer vowels and consonants in languages that are not in their environment • More and more patterns in the languages they hear • Some words pronounced slowly and clearly	• Repetitive babbling using sounds of languages in the environment • Long strings of babbling with adult-like intonation • Word-like utterances that may have several meanings • Some musical notes
12–18 months	• Categories and nuances of words • Words within phrases • Short phrases	• First word (differing from language to language) • Naming explosion or "word spurt" • Repeating, shouting, interjecting
18–24 months	• Awareness of language • Order of words in phrases • Increasingly complex words and phrases	• "Telegraphic speech" with word order appropriate to the particular language • Consonants t, k, b, d, g, n, m, f, s, h, and w

Do "Green Eggs and Ham" Again!

Newborns respond to prose they heard as fetuses. Researchers Anthony DeCasper and Melanie Spence asked expectant mothers to read a passage to their babies every day during the last six weeks of pregnancy. Soon after the children were born, a third person read two passages to the babies: the passage they had heard in utero and a new selection with a different rhythm. The infants, sucking on a non-nutritive nipple, sucked at different rates for the different passages, clearly indicating that they could hear the different rhythms. They preferred the passage that their mother had read to them in utero.

ence between the vowels in *vue* and *vous* in French, and virtually all of the speech sounds in the world. If your baby is listening to the sounds of Spanish, she will hear all of the nuances in the entire Spanish sound inventory.

Faces and voices

Your new baby is listening intently, looking at mouths, and imitating, all of which are helpful in learning to speak. She is fascinated and comforted by voices. In fact, her first smile will be a response to hearing a voice. She knows her mother's voice and, possibly, her father's. She is now becoming acquainted with the voices and faces of the remaining cast of characters in her world. Slow speech with short words is easiest for her to process.

WHAT YOUR BABY IS SAYING FROM BIRTH TO 6 MONTHS

Reflexive sounds

The birth cry signals the beginning of your baby's speech development. She is now ready

39

to master any language in the world. The first vocalizations your child produces are reflexes. She will cry, fuss, and produce vegetative sounds. Many of the first non-distress sounds to emerge are rather nasal-sounding. The nasality of early sounds is largely due to the anatomical structure of an infant's vocal tract. It is smaller and more linear than the adult's—much more like a nonhuman primate's. As your baby gains more control over her tongue and lips, she will produce sounds such as *ogoo* and gurgly noises. At eight weeks, she might coo when she feels cozy and when you smile or talk to her.

Voluntary sounds

Your baby produces her first non-reflexive sounds when she is playing with adults. Sounds that were previously produced as reflexes are now combined with vowel-like sounds and produced non-reflexively. She might also put her lips together, giving rise to some *m* or *b* sounds during play.

Close to the six-month period, your baby is exploring her mouth and voice with abandon, growling, yelling, and producing other entertaining sounds. Much to your chagrin, she wonders how loudly she can scream, whether she can reach that high C, and what happens when she puts her lips together and blows. She will talk to herself and practice vocalizing with her loved ones. Only by approximately six months of age (coinciding with the beginning of babbling) has her vocal tract arranged itself into the angle configuration found in adults. Now her sounds will be even more adult-like.

Communication

Although she does not have words, she communicates by gazing, touching, and vocalizing. She converses, not just attempting to repeat what she hears, but creating her own utterances. She smiles back at you, "talks" back, and laughs along with you. Laughter serves important developmental (as well as social) functions. It requires rapid starting and stopping movement of vocal cords— necessary skills for producing consonants.

FROM SIX MONTHS TO A YEAR

WHAT YOUR BABY IS HEARING FROM SIX TO TWELVE MONTHS

Sound distinctions lost

From six months to a year, dramatic changes take place in children's perception of foreign sounds. As infants become increasingly sensitive to sounds of their own language or languages, their perceptual skills in languages they do not hear demonstrate a rapid decline. At this point, most categories of sounds are being established for the languages in the baby's environment. If she is hearing enough Spanish long *r* sounds, she is establishing a special long *r*-category in her Spanish inventory. Now, your task is to keep those categories active so that they are maintained. These are good months for immersion *en espaol*, and active use of the *Baby's First Steps* CD. If she is not exposed to sounds of a foreign language during this stage, she will lose her sensitivity to many of the sounds.

The perceptual changes may be reversible; that is, her sensitivity might be regained, but only if the language reenters her life within the next few years, and certainly before puberty.

Already by seven-and-a-half months, your baby is beginning to pick out words she hears frequently in fluent speech. (Words will be emphasized on the *Baby's First Steps* CD in Spanish "parentese" for her processing ease.) Words in English she might notice are *cup, shoe, juice* and other commonly used words. She may understand *no, hot*, and some simple commands, and respond when you call her name.

WHAT YOUR BABY IS SAYING FROM SIX TO TWELVE MONTHS

"Babababababa": Canonical babbling

While your six-month-old explores her mouth and voice, she may press her lips together, then open her mouth wide. That will be fun, so she will do it again. Soon sounds emerge:

41

Divi dingsen tences

Language is a flowing stream of sounds. Listeners need to determine how to segment or break up sentences into the words. In his entertaining book on linguistics, *The Language Instinct,* Steven Pinker provides some examples of segmenting gone awry, which has happened to all of us listening to lyrics of songs. For example, listening to the song "Lucy in the Sky with Diamonds" by the Beatles, "A girl with kaleidoscope eyes" was segmented as "A girl with colitis goes by." Computers have notorious difficulty breaking down sentences, and even clearly-pronounced words. Yet somehow, six-month-old infants are already tackling this task quite successfully.

ma-ma, pa-pa. You jump with joy, thrilled that she is calling your name.

The disappointing news is that at this babbling stage, she is probably not calling her mother or father—the sounds *mama, dada*, and *papa* are universally among the most common first babblings. Babies all over the world produce syllables that begin with a consonant and end with a vowel (e.g., *ma*). The first consonants uttered are usually produced when their lips come together (e.g., *b, p,* or *m*),

and the vowels are produced with a wide-open mouth (e.g., *a*). As your baby's coordination develops, she will move the tip of her tongue to the roof of her mouth to say, "dada" or move the back of her tongue to say, "gaga." These sounds are repetitive, hence the name "canonical" babbling.

The wonderful news, however, is that babbling is truly a milestone in language development. Your child is producing utterances that have the timing and structure of adult syllables. With her building blocks of syllables, she will soon create words. Within months, she might say, and actually mean, "mama," "dada," and "cu" (for *cup*).

Babbling in different languages

Babies babble differently in different languages. In an experiment by the researcher Bénédicte de Boysson-Bardies, French adults had no trouble identifying whether eight-month-old babblers were French or foreign. The listeners pointed to intonation and rhythm as their clues to the children's native language. Relative to other babblers, ten-month-old English children produce more vowels that sound like *eeh*, and French speakers produce more vowels with pursed lips (e.g., the vowel in French *vue* "view" or *feu* "fire"). Clearly, infants are not just *perceiving* vowels in the languages in their environment with more accuracy than vowels in other languages—they are already *producing* vowels of their surrounding languages, and producing them accurately.

"Duubeegaa guu grrrraaa": Jargon

Canonical babbling with repeated syllables (e.g., "bababa") generally extends from approximately six to ten months. Toward the end of this stage, your baby will vary her vowels and consonants more and more as she plays. She is beginning to engage in "jargon," that is, produce utterances that sound like sentences, but are made with nonsense syllables and words. She might proclaim, "Duubeegaa guu grrrraaa," for example. She may produce long strings of such jargon, commenting extensively, giving a speech, or asking questions. What she is doing, in fact, is practicing the rhythm, melody, and speech sounds she hears when you talk and, also communicating messages without actually using words. Soon her utterances will begin to contain word-like forms.

"Baaak": Word-like utterances

Starting at about ten or twelve months, word-like utterances will bridge the gap between babbling and first words. Your child may produce a recurrent form that bears no apparent resemblance to any adult word. She might say, "baaak" every time she wants a toy, for example. She will have less difficulty gesturing than communicating through speech. This ease with gesture is one reason babies love songs that include hand movements (e.g., "Wheels on the Bus," "Itsy-Bitsy-Spider," or several of the songs on the attached CD). You might even be able to persuade her to sing a few notes as she gestures.

FROM TWELVE MONTHS TO EIGHTEEN MONTHS

WHAT YOUR BABY IS HEARING FROM TWELVE TO EIGHTEEN MONTHS

Your child's main linguistic challenge around her first birthday is learning words—that is, learning to match sounds she hears with concepts she knows. Swiss child psychologist Jean Piaget discussed the first two years of life as the period of "sensorimotor intelligence." Infants develop the important notion that objects exist, even if they are hidden, and begin to have internal mental representations or concepts of objects (hence the universally loved, endlessly played game of "peekaboo"). With a more stable concept of objects, children understand that names are consistently applied to similar objects. This revelation will enable your baby to learn words. With this notion of "object permanence" and more control of her mouth and tongue, she will produce one word, then another, and by the end of this period, she may have fifty words.

It takes exposure to objects and words in many contexts for children to understand the boundaries of word meanings. A child learning two languages faces challenges when words in both languages have slightly different meanings. For example, the word *ruka* in Russian denotes the part of the body that extends from the hand to the top of the arm, whereas in English the word *hand* is just the part with a wrist and fingers and the rest is the *arm*. Bilingual Russian/English children will discover not only that two words exist for this same general area, but also exactly what each term encompasses.

First words

The first spoken word universally occurs at approximately one year of age, and the next six months will witness an explosion of approximately fifty more. Your child's first words will probably refer to things that are present in the environment and things that move. *Shoes, car,* and *bottle* are common first words in English.

"Doti": Pronouncing first words

Parents might have difficulty understanding their children's first words. For example, a one-year-old might pronounce *doggie* as "doti." Pronunciation for several sounds is unlikely to be adult-like until approximately the age of four, since the sound system and fine motor skills required for speech take years to be fine-tuned. Your child might say *cu* or even *tu* for *cup*. She will tend to simplify words so

Different first words in different countries

The language acquisition expert Bénédicte de Boysson-Bardies interviewed babies in several countries to determine what types of words would be found in those whose vocabularies consisted of fewer than 50 words.

Americans were active namers, naming people around them, cartoon characters, and characters in nursery rhymes. American babies were more interested in things than in actions: A large proportion of the words they uttered were nouns. This was thought to be due to American parents' emphasis on pointing to things and naming them: hopefully not a reflection of the children's value systems.

Perhaps not surprisingly, French babies talked about food quite a bit more than other children. Although their gustatorial vocabulary was approximately the same, French babies made more use of the words.

Japanese children had fewer nouns than other groups, concentrating more on nature (e.g., *rain*, *leaf*, and *moon*) than on toys or foods. Lovely onomatopoetic forms (words that sound like what they denote, e.g., *buzz* in English) made up more than half of the Japanese children's words. Babies said, "jaja" for the sound of water, "kon kon" for banging a hammer, "kira kira" for the sparkle of light.

Across the different languages, polite phrases had already been learned by most children, e.g., *thank you* and *let's shake hands*, and *haro* in Japanese, a loan-word from English meaning "hello," clearly borrowed after the critical period for learning sounds!

they are easier to pronounce. She might leave off consonants at the end of a syllable (e.g., *ba* for *ball*), and delete entire syllables (e.g., *coo* for *cookie*).

FROM EIGHTEEN TO TWENTY-FOUR MONTHS

WHAT YOUR BABY IS HEARING FROM EIGHTEEN TO TWENTY-FOUR MONTHS

From words to phrases

At eighteen months, your baby is learning approximately four new words a day. She is organizing words into categories, an excellent tool for increasing her vocabulary. She identifies several body parts, items to eat, and items to wear. She is also paying close attention to phrases and to the order of words in a phrase, noticing that, in English, people say "black shoes," and not "shoes black." Without knowing what nouns and adjectives are, she is learning that an adjective is followed by a noun in English. If she is surrounded by

Spanish, she is also learning that for that language the opposite is usually the case. She uses context to help her make sense of what you are saying, relying on what is happening in the environment to figure out what your words mean.

Awareness of language

Around the age of two, your baby becomes aware of language. If you do not understand something she says, she might try to say it differently, understanding that language is separate from the message, and that the same thing can be said in several ways. (The last section of the *Baby's First Steps* CD focuses on linguistic awareness.) As we discovered in the "Multilingualism" chapter, this awareness occurs more extensively in multilingual children. Mélina, the bilingual toddler, would say "English," and then make funny, English *r*-like sounds, indicating that that was what English sounded like to her. This awareness helps children develop all of their languages and aids them in reading and writing them.

Mini-sentences

Soon, your baby will put two words together and form her first mini-sentence. At approximately eighteen months, she will develop "telegraphic speech," using just the most important words to convey her thoughts. Remarkably, children produce the word order that is appropriate in their language. For example, your child might say, "Elmo run," or "Big kitty." Words might be missing, but the order is adult-like. Similarly, children learning Spanish abide by Spanish word order and also by complex grammatical rules of the language (e.g., using feminine adjectives with feminine nouns).

Your baby's phrases will continue to increase in size, so that, at thirty months, she will have an average sentence length of approximately three words. Her spoken vocabulary will have 250 to 300 words by the time she is two, allowing her to use various combinations to comment, persuade, respond, and ask questions.

Overgeneralization: I runned

Children will begin to "overgeneralize," that is, apply grammatical rules of their language to words that might not be appropriate. For example, your child might say, "taked" for *took*, "runned" for *ran*, "goed" for *went*, and "eated" for *ate*. You need not correct your child. For one thing, it will not help. If your child says, "I runned to the park," and you say, "Ran, dear," she will probably say, "Yeah, I runned to the park."

Furthermore, overgeneralization is a good sign, highly admired by linguists and speech pathologists all over the world. It indicates that your child has learned an important aspect of her language. In the case of "runned," she learned that adding -*ed* creates a past tense. Soon enough, she will allow exceptions to her rule, and will ultimately say "ran," much to your relief.

"I tee you": Normal pronunciation errors

Your child will use many of the sound patterns she has been aware of in your speech. As she produces the sounds she has perceived, she is expected to make errors. By the age of two, a typical inventory includes *t, k, b, d, g, n, m, f, s, h,* and *w* at the beginning of syllables in English. Patterns of errors will tend to be systematic within a child. For example, if your child says, "I tee you," instead of "I see you," she is likely to substitute *t* for *s* in other words, as well, and say, "tee-taw" for *see-saw*. Your child is learning regularities of sounds, sound combinations, and language, and testing her hypotheses. She might be practicing sounds in Spanish by now, imitating sounds on the CD, attempting to "roll" the *r*, and so forth. The next chapter, "Making the Most of the CD," will give you ideas about how to encourage her participation.

5. Making the Most of the CD

Children learn concepts and speech patterns most easily when they are combined with music. This is the basis for the early acquisition of commercial jingles or the popularity of alphabet songs.

—SUZANNE EVANS MORRIS IN *MARVELOUS MOUTH MUSIC*

THE CONCEPT BEHIND THE CD

*T*he *Baby's First Steps* CD provides Spanish sounds, words, and sentences at a time when they are most likely to leave an indelible mark on your child's perceptual system. Children learn and remember sounds best in combination with music and poetry; thus traditional Spanish children's songs and poems are included. Variations on the traditional lyrics reflect the sound inventory of Spanish—building on and emphasizing sounds that are especially relevant at your child's particular stage of development. Emphasis involves techniques that are effective teaching tools: slow and clear production of sounds ("parentese"), repetition, and playful variations that entice your baby to vocalize.

AN INVITATION

*J*ust listening to the CD gives your baby a world of sounds he might otherwise not hear and lets him internalize a sound system that may help him learn Spanish and other languages later in life. Although the CD is useful on its own, you are invited to interact with your baby while playing the selections and thereby enhance the benefits of the Spanish sounds. When your child is engaged and motivated, he will interact with the material and absorb the information better. You are encouraged to engage your child in vocal play, singing, and tapping. The suggestions below will help you bring out the important lessons in the selections and simultaneously make the CD more entertaining and enjoyable for your baby and you.

THE STRUCTURE OF THE CD

*T*he CD is divided into four sections corresponding to the first four six-month periods of your baby's development. The songs, rhymes, and speech sounds have been carefully designed to emphasize the important aspects of Spanish that your child is uniquely open to absorbing at each developmental stage. Each section contains all the sounds in the Spanish inventory so that your child may continue to perceive them accurately.

WHEN TO PLAY THE CD

*Y*ou are encouraged to play selections frequently from your child's birth until he turns one. This crucial first year of life is when sound categories are being formed in your child's mind. Thus, if he is to continue to perceive Spanish sounds with "perfect pitch," he must be exposed to them regularly for at least his first year of life.

You are welcome to play the entire CD at any time during (and after) your baby's first two years of life. But if you prefer just to play a few selections, it is best to choose those that are designed for your child's particular stage of development. Preferably, selections should be played at least three times a week,

THE FOUR SECTIONS OF THE CD

1. Rhythm and oohs: Newborn to 6 months

The first section emphasizes the even rhythm of Spanish and all of the Spanish vowels and consonants, as your baby is keenly sensitive to the rhythms and sounds of all languages. Within this section (as in each of the sections), the entire inventory of Spanish sounds will be presented. Vowels will receive special attention, as these are some of the first sounds infants begin to have difficulty perceiving.

2. Oohs and aahs: 6 to 12 months

This stage is crucial for retaining all of the speech sounds in the Spanish inventory. This section emphasizes the vowels and consonants that are particularly vulnerable to loss as babies grow attuned to their native language. Babies are also beginning to understand the concept of words; thus, words will be emphasized alone and in phrases.

3. Words of wisdom: 12 to 18 months

This is the stage of words, words, and more words. This section of the CD brings out important words: body parts, categories such as fruits and numbers, and so forth. Sounds will continue to be emphasized so that your baby's inventory of Spanish consonants and vowels remains well-stocked.

4. Aha—language! 18 to 24 months

Your baby has begun to notice that two words exist for one object: one in English and one in Spanish. Language awareness will help your child improve his language skills and even his reading skills in the future. Your child is also paying close attention to the order of words in phrases. Thus, Spanish words, phrases, and sentences characterize this section.

although it is understood that babies profit more from repetition than do their parents! As long as you interact with your baby and the selections, he will continue to make gains in his processing of foreign sounds and words.

HOW TO PARTICIPATE

YOUR GENERAL APPROACH

Sounds that infants hear effortlessly must often be explicitly taught to their parents, and the teaching is never perfect. The next chapter, "The Sounds of Spanish," gives you tips on how you can better hear and produce Spanish sounds so that you can be a knowledgeable participant in your baby's education (and take advantage of a little Spanish practice yourself!).

You are welcome to participate as much or as little as you like, although, as we have seen, more is better. Feel free to sing along, talk along, and clap along. It is harmless, and probably enjoyable, for your baby to hear your attempts at foreign sounds. In fact, the more

entertaining the ad-libbing you do, the more motivated your baby will be to join in. You are encouraged to be yourself and enjoy the adventure.

However, if you are not a native speaker of Spanish, you are probably not producing the sounds with one hundred percent accuracy, so you should be careful not to consistently cover up the sounds on the tape with your own production. If your not-quite-accurate version consistently hides the accurate Spanish pronunciation on the CD, your child will not be exposed to the sounds he needs to hear. You might consider yourself a facilitator between your baby and the CD—pointing out and contributing important information, but still letting your child converse with the CD.

SUGGESTIONS FOR EACH STAGE

RHYTHM AND OOHS: NEWBORN TO 6 MONTHS

You are encouraged to tap out rhythms (by tapping the crib, shaking a rattle, or clapping). Rock your baby, sing along gently, and invite him into the world of Spanish sounds. For some of the poems, it is traditional to bounce your baby up and down on your lap or tickle him. Feel free to join in the tradition. As you listen to the foreign language "parentese," add your own "parentese" in English once in a while, using rising and falling intonation. Your baby will compare and contrast the different sounds he hears.

OOHS AND AAHS: 6 TO 12 MONTHS

Play the CD most during this crucial stage in maintenance of foreign sounds. Pucker your lips and attempt quiet pronunciations when you hear sounds like *ooh*—this might encourage your baby to try some sounds. Open your mouth wide and pretend to yawn when you hear *ahhh*. Try to make the *r* sound in silly ways, and make entertaining sounds to keep your baby engaged in the interesting sounds.

WORDS OF WISDOM: 12 TO 18 MONTHS

You may emphasize the words within the songs by pointing to objects that correspond to any Spanish words you might understand. Point to different body parts on your baby or to different fruits when you hear them mentioned. You might also want to cut out pictures of apples, for example, so you can refer to the pictures when you hear the words. When you hear animal noises in Spanish, produce the English equivalent and point to your dog or to a picture of a dog, for example. Count on your fingers or on your baby's fingers when you hear counting in Spanish.

AHA—LANGUAGE! 18 TO 24 MONTHS

Here your child is learning linguistic awareness—that there are different ways to say the same thing. Pointing to pictures and objects continues to be important, but now you can be explicit in communicating that the sounds on the CD are Spanish and that your sounds are English. You might say the name of the object in English when you hear it in Spanish. And say "español" while listening intently to the CD; then "English" when you say something in English. The sounds, then, continue to be emphasized. You might want to attempt to imitate several of them, exaggerating and being silly as you articulate. Your child might be singing a little and attempting his own imitations at this point. Mutual encouragement will keep both of you engaged and learning Spanish sounds.

6. The Sounds of Spanish

IN THIS CHAPTER, YOU WILL DISCOVER . . .

★ SPANISH WORD FORMS
★ WHAT DIFFERENTIATES SOUNDS FROM LETTERS
★ HOW TO PRONOUNCE SPANISH VOWELS AND CONSONANTS
★ DIFFERENCES BETWEEN SPANISH AND ENGLISH SOUNDS
★ PRONUNCIATION TECHNIQUES FOR THE MORE DIFFICULT SOUNDS
★ HOW TO PRACTICE THE RHYTHM AND MELODY OF SPANISH

*L*et's look at some of the sound characteristics of the Spanish language, and let's contrast these sounds with those that we produce in English. The comparisons between Spanish and English will help you understand—and hopefully avoid—common errors typically made by English speakers.

THE SHAPE OF WORDS IN SPANISH AND THE TIMING IN PRONUNCIATION

*M*ost words in Spanish are made up of two or more syllables, whereas in English, one-syllable words, such as *prince, house,* or *stairs* are common. Consider the Spanish equivalents of these words: *principe, casa, escalera.* You can see that the words in Spanish are longer. You will also notice that in Spanish, all the letters are pronounced, whereas in English, several letters appear to be silent or are less "stressed." This is an important characteristic of Spanish, and one that will facilitate your learning of the language: you can trust the Spanish spelling. Once you learn the sounds of the letters in Spanish, you will find that the pronunciation of most words can be predicted from the way they are spelled.

Syllables in Spanish contain at most two consonants preceding a vowel; however, in English, three or more consonants are not uncommon. While most Spanish words consist of simply a vowel (V), consonant + vowel (CV), or vowel + consonant (VC) syllable structure, you will also find syllables made up of two consonants plus a vowel (CCV), such as in *pla-to* "dish." In Spanish, the only consonants allowed at the end of words or at the end of syllables are: [s], [r], [n], [l], and [d]. Therefore, in a CVC combination, the final letter will always be one of the above consonants, e.g., *can-tar* "sing," *e-dad* "age,"

ses-tos "baskets." In Spanish, you may also find two adjacent vowels, which are separated into two distinct syllables in pronunciation, e.g., *re-ír* "to laugh," *o-ír* "to hear," *ma-iz* "corn."

There is another, more important difference between English and Spanish. In Spanish, most syllables are pronounced with equal timing, even when stress is assigned to only one of the syllables within the word. Say the word *es-ca-le-ra*: be careful to place the stress on the third syllable, but pronounce each syllable with equal timing. In English, syllables with weak stress are given less time in pronunciation and their vowels are "reduced" or pronounced as an *uh* sound. You can test this characteristic of English by saying aloud the following words: *telephone; computer*. Notice now the difference in Spanish by pronouncing the equivalent words (be careful to assign equal timing to each syllable and to pronounce every letter): *telefono; computadora*.

SOUNDS, NOT LETTERS: THE INTERNATIONAL PHONETIC ALPHABET (IPA)

*D*epicting the "sounds" of a language is not an easy task. You may ask whether that is what we do when we write words. While this is true, there are important exceptions. First of all, any language has more "sounds" than "letters," and in many cases more than one sound is assigned per letter. Think of the words *come* and *cent*—both words are spelled with the letter "c," but in the first one, the sound is [k], and in the second one, the sound is [s]. The same is found in Spanish in words *cama* "bed" and *centro* "center." The first word is pronounced as [kama], and the second one is pronounced as [sentro].

In order to represent the sounds of a language with precision, a set of special symbols, called the International Phonetic Alphabet (IPA), was created. In most dictionaries, you will notice that next to each word entry, there are brackets, [ ], containing symbols that are not always familiar. These are the IPA symbols, and they are showing you how to pronounce the word. We use these symbols to differentiate the "sounds" from the "letters."

LAS VOCALES: THE SPANISH VOWELS

*W*e know that when learning another language, mastering the sounds is quite challenging. However, you should know that as an English-speaker, you may have an advantage in learning the sounds of Spanish. Why could this be so? Well, in Spanish, there are only five vowel sounds to be mastered, while fifteen vowel sounds are used in English. Furthermore, the five vowel sounds in Spanish always correspond to the same vowel letters, so that there is absolutely no confusion. Let's look at these vowel sounds and try to find their equivalents in English.

Remember from the previous section that Spanish is what language specialists call "a syllable-timed" language. Keep this in mind as you practice Spanish words, and pay special attention to vowels, as they are responsi-

SPANISH VOWELS			
SOUND	**EXAMPLE**	**DESCRIPTION**	**SPANISH SPELLING**
[a]	mama	Similar to *a* in English *father*	a
[e]	tete	Similar to *a* in *fate* but cut off	e
[i]	si	Similar to *i* in *machine*	i
[o]	no	Similar to *o* in *note* but cut off	o
[u]	tu	Similar as the *u* in *rude*	u

ble for the syllabic structure and the timing in the pronunciation of words.

One note of caution on the pronunciation of the letter "u" in Spanish: it should remain silent when found between the letters "g" and "e" or "g" and "i," as in the words *guerra* [geRa] and *guiso* [giso]. It should also remain silent when found between the letters "q" and "e" and "q" and "i," e.g., *queso* [keso] and *quimera* [kimera].

HOW CONSONANTS ARE PRODUCED

$\mathcal{I}$n many language, consonants are produced differently from vowels. Vowels are pronounced with minimal obstruction from the tongue or lips, so that the "voice" travels quite freely from your vocal cords and out of your mouth to become the sound of the words you pronounce. In contrast, consonants are produced by obstructing or stopping the air stream exiting your lungs as you speak. For instance, in the case of [p], your lips come together twice in the word *papá* "daddy." In the case of [s], the tongue "narrows" the air passage, producing the characteristic "wind-like" sound we find in a word such as *sister*. Can you tell where the obstruction lies for sounds such as [f], [m], [l], and [k] by looking

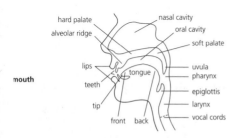

mouth

at the drawing of the mouth enclosed?

Some consonants are "voiced" because your vocal cords vibrate as you pronounce them, as in the case of *b, d,* or *z.* Place the palm of your hand on your throat and feel the vibrations: this is the "voicing" that is added to the airstream as it comes up from your lungs and exits your mouth to become a sound. Other consonants are "devoiced" because they do not carry the vibration from your vocal cords. For all consonants, the airstream is obstructed at various points in the mouth, and it is mainly this "obstructing action" that produces the sound. In English, the "obstruction" or "stopping" of some consonants is very strong and causes an explosive "turbulence" at the point where the airstream is interrupted (e.g., *p, t,* and *k* sounds). Think of the word *pop,* and you will notice this turbulence, which is also called "aspiration." This is a phonetic feature that you will not find in Spanish.

LAS CONSONANTES: SPANISH CONSONANTS

*M*ost consonants in Spanish are pronounced in much the same way as those in English. However, there are some consonants in Spanish that are different from or do not exist in English, such as [ɲ], spelled "ñ," which is similar to the sound of "ni" in *onion.* On the other hand, in Spanish we find the [tʃ] sound (as in the word *chair*), but there is no [ʃ] sound (as in the word *sheep*). When a sound is not present in our native language, the natural tendency for us is to find its closest equivalent. This is why many Spanish speakers, trying to learn English, pronounce *Washington* as [watʃinton]. There are some subtle differences in the way some consonants are pronounced in Spanish when we compare them with their equivalents in English, and knowing these differences helps to avoid pronunciation errors in Spanish. The table of Spanish consonants is given on page 62.

....

[B]RRRRR: THE TRILLED *R* IN SPANISH

....

The name of the character Zorro and the distinct way in which [R] is pronounced in his name typify some of the characteristics of this sound in Spanish. This "strong" sound may be difficult for someone whose native language is English. Actually, the [R] sound is possibly the one that varies the most in the dialects of Spanish that are spoken in different parts of the globe. For instance, in Puerto Rico, the "trilling" is produced by raising the back portion of the tongue, so that the sound is closer to [h]. For the sake of simplicity, we will practice here the trilled [R] that is typical of Spain. The fact that [R] is so variously produced may point to the fact that it is a difficult sound, and that it has undergone "simplification" in many countries. So do not feel discouraged if producing [R] requires extra practice. You should also know that the [R] sound is trilled at the beginning of words, e.g., *risa* [Risa], in the middle syllable, e.g., *perro* [peRo], and following the consonants [l], [s], and [n], e.g., *alrededor* [alRededor], *Israel* [isRael], *enredo* [enRedo].

The simple [r] sound in Spanish is found in middle syllables, e.g., *perico* [periko], and following consonants other than [l], [s], and [n]. Practice saying the following words with a simple [r] sound, which is similar to the sound represented by the letters "tt" in English words *butter, potter*, and *mutter*: [broma], [presion], [franko], [dragon], [grano], [krono], [trono].

THE SOUNDS OF SPANISH

SPANISH CONSONANTS

SOUND	EXAMPLE	DESCRIPTION	SPANISH SPELLING
[b]	bola	Similar to b in *ball*	b, v
[β]	cabo	There is no exact equivalent in English, but it approximates v as in *verse*	b, v, between vowels
[ð]	vida	There is no exact equivalent in English, but think of *th* in *mother*	d
[f]	fiesta	Similar to f in *fire*	f
[g]	goma	Similar to g in *gold*	g
[ɣ]	pago	There is no exact equivalent in English, but think of the sound g as a bridge connecting two vowels	g, between vowels
[h]	jota	Similar to h in *hole*	j, g + i, e
[j]	yo	Similar to y in *yes*	y, ll
[k]	copa	Similar to c in *cat*	c, k, q
[l]	lobo	Similar to l in *love*	l
[m]	mas	Similar to m in *more*	m
[n]	no	Similar to n in *note*	n
[ŋ]	cinco	Similar to *ng* in *sing*	n, before c, q, k or g
[ɲ]	niña	Similar to *ni* in *onion*	ñ
[p]	pelota	Similar to p in *spot*	p

SPANISH CONSONANTS (CONTINUED)			
SOUND	EXAMPLE	DESCRIPTION	SPANISH SPELLING
[r]	oro	There is no exact equivalent in English, but think of the sound of *tt* in *butter*	r
[R]	perro	There is no equivalent in English. The [R] sound is produced by trilling or tapping the tip of your tongue rapidly against the hard palate as a steady stream of air is pushed out (similar to making an engine noise).	rr
[s]	sapo	Similar to *s* in *second*	s, z, c + e, i
[t]	tango	Similar to *t* in *stop*	t
[tʃ]	chiste	Similar to *ch* in *chair*	ch
[θ][4]	zapato	There is no equivalent in English, but think of *th* in *thumb*	z, c + i, e

SPANISH IS A MELODY: RHYTHM AND INTONATION

$\mathcal{W}$e pointed out earlier that while in English, syllables alternate between strong and weak or reduced, in Spanish, syllables maintain more equal length whether stressed or not. This is such an important characteristic of the rhythmic pattern of Spanish that

---

[4] Note that this sound is typical of European Spanish pronunciation. In Latin American Spanish, it is always rendered as an *s* sound.

THE SOUNDS OF SPANISH

the language is often described as a language with an even rhythm or a "syllable-timed" language.

We know that learning the "rhythm" and the "intonation" of a language can add much to the fluency with which words are spoken. Listen to a Spanish newscaster in a radio or television show, and try to capture the "melody" of the language. You will notice that it is very distinct. It is this distinctiveness in the "melody" or the "rhythm and intonation" of a language that allows you to differentiate among unfamiliar languages. You can test this by thinking of the intonation patterns of dissimilar languages such as French, German, and Italian.

Remember that infants learn to speak by first perceiving and then producing intonation patterns of their native languages. We mentioned earlier that babies babble strings of syllables that sound like entire monologues and do not contain a single word! Your baby will capture the melody of the language before producing any words. So feel free to expose your child to "spoken" Spanish on the CD, and on Spanish radio and television. Enjoy your own growing ability to communicate in Spanish and appreciate the richness of the culture. You, your baby, and your entire family are ready to embark on an enriching and fascinating linguistic adventure. *¡Buen viaje!*

Resources for Parents

BOOKS

The following books require no linguistic background and provide plenty of research-based information.

A Parents' and Teachers' Guide to Bilingualism. Baker, C., Clevedon, England: Multilingual Matters, Ltd., 2000.

How Language Comes to Children: From Birth to Two Years. Boysson-Bardies, B. de. London: MIT Press, 1999.

How Babies Talk. Golinkoff, R.M. & Hirsh-Pasek, K. New York: Dutton, 1999.

The Scientist in the Crib: Minds, Brains, and How Children Learn. Gopnik, A., Meltzoff, A.N., & Kuhl, P.K. New York: William Morrow, 1999.

These are some highly recommended and accessible offerings from the academic world.

Speech Perception and Linguistic Experience: Issues in Cross-language Research. Strange, W. ed., Timonium, Maryland: York Press, 1995.

The Exceptional Brain: Neuropsychology of Talent and Special Abilities. Obler, L.K. & Fein, D. eds. New York: The Guilford Press, 1988.

INTERNET SITES

These are some well-informed Web sites where you can learn more about language, bilingual children and adults, and foreign languages.

For resources for parents thinking about raising their child bilingually:

Bilingual Parenting Web site
www.byu.edu
(link to bilingualism/index.html)

For a wealth of sources for foreign-language—related information and products:

Clearinghouse for Multicultural/Bilingual Education
www.weber.edu/MBE

ERIC, a non-profit clearinghouse site on languages and linguistics, offers services for parents and bilingual educators.

ERIC, Clearinghouse on Languages and Linguistics
www.cal.org (link to Clearinghouse/Eric)

For a catalogue of language-related Internet resources with numerous links:

Human Languages Page
www.june29.com

For information and FAQs about language for both academics and non-academics:

Linguistic Society of America
www.lsadc.org

The following is a site for the publisher of journals about multiculturalism and multilingualism. Books on related topics for parents and teachers can be bought, and useful links are provided.

Multilingual Matters and Channel View Publications
www.multilingual-matters.com

References

INTRODUCTION TO PACKAGE

Polka, O. & Werker, J.F. Developmental Changes in Perception of Non-Native Contrasts. *Journal of Experimental Psychology: Human Perception and Performance* 20 (1994): 421–435.

Tees, R.C. & Werker, J.F. Perceptual Flexibility: Maintenance or Recovery of the Ability to Discriminate Non-native Speech Sounds. *Canadian Journal of Psychology* 38 (1984): (4), 579–590.

Werker, J.F. & Tees, R.C. Cross-language Speech Perception: Evidence for Perceptual Reorganization During Their First Year of Life. *Infant Behavior and Development* 7 (1984): 49–63.

CHAPTER I: CRITICAL PERIODS FOR BIRDS AND BABIES

Bruer, J.T. *The Myth of the First Three Years: A New Understanding of Early Brain Development and Lifelong Learning.* New York: The Free Press, 1999.

Flege, J.E. Second Language Speech Learning: Theory, Findings, and Problems. In Strange, W. ed., *Speech Perception and Linguistic Experience: Issues in Cross-language Research* (Timonium, Maryland: York Press, 1995), 233–277.

Fromkin. V. & Rodman, R. *An Introduction to Language*. Fort Worth, Texas: Harcourt Brace & Co, 1998.

Johnson, J.S. & Newport, E.L. Critical Periods Effects in Second-language Learning: The Influence of Maturational State on the Acquisition of English as a

Second Language. *Cognitive Psychology* 21 (1989): 60–99.

Kim, K. S., Relkin, N., Lee, K.M., & Hirsch, J. Distinct Cortical Areas Associated with Native and Second Languages. *Nature.* 388 (1997): 171–174.

Kuhl, P.K., Williams, K.A., Lacerda, F., Stevens, K.N., & Lindblom, B. Linguistic Experience Alters Phonetic Perception in Infants by 6 Months of Age. *Science* 255 (1992): 606–608.

Levy, E.S., Goral, M., & Obler, L.K. Neurolinguistic Perspectives on Mother Tongue: Evidence from Aphasia and Brain Imaging. *Les Cahiers Charles V,* 27. Paris: Publication de l'Université de Paris 7, 1999.

Lorenz, K.Z. *Evolution and the Modification of Behavior*, Chicago: University of Chicago Press, 1965.

Marler, P. A Comparative Approach to Vocal Learning: Song Development in White-crowned Sparrows. *J. Comp. Physiol. Psychol. Monograph* 71 (1970): 1–25.

Margoliash, D. Neural Plasticity in Birdsong Learning, in Rauschecker, J.P. & Marler, P.

eds., *Imprinting and Cortical Plasticity: Comparative Aspects of Sensitive Periods* New York: John Wiley & Sons,1987, 23–54.

Polka, O. & Werker, J.F. Developmental Changes in Perception of Non-Native Vowel Contrasts. *Journal of Experimental Psychology: Human Perception and Performance* 20 (1994): 421–435.

Shatz, C.J. The Developing Brain. *Scientific American* (September 1992): 61.

Strange, W. ed. *Speech Perception and Linguistic Experience: Issues in Cross-language Research.* Timonium, Maryland: York Press, 1995.

Werker, J.F. & Tees, R.C. Cross Language Speech Perception: Evidence for Perceptual Reorganization During the First Year of Life. *Infant Behavior and Development* 7 (1984): 49–63.

CHAPTER II: HELPING YOUR TINY TALKER TALK

Baker, C. *A Parents' and Teachers' Guide to Bilingualism.* Clevedon, England: Multilingual Matters, Ltd., 2000.

Chomsky, N. A Review of Skinner's "Verbal Behavior." *Language* 35 (1959): 26–58.

Einstein, A. Letter to Sybille Blinoff, May 21 in Fölsing, A., *Albert Einstein: A Biography*. Translated by Ewald Osers. New York: Penguin Books, 1997.

Leach, P. *Your Baby and Child: From Birth to Age Five.* New York: Knopf, 1997.

Snow, C. & Ferguson, C. *Talking to Children: Language Input and Acquisition*. New York: Cambridge University Press, 1977.

CHAPTER III: MULTILINGUALISM

Bialystok, E. Children's Concept of Word. *Journal of Psycholinguistic Research* 15 (1986): 13–22.

Cook, V. The Consequences of Bilingualism for Cognitive Processing. In De Groot, A.M.B. & Kroll, J.F. eds., *Tutorials in Bilingualism: Psycholinguistic Perspectives.* New Jersey: Lawrence Erlbaum Associates, Inc., 1997.

Grosjean, F. *Life with Two Languages: An Introduction to Bilingualism*. Cambridge, Massachusetts: Cambridge University Press, 1982.

Kroll, J.F. & Stewart, E. Category Interference in Translation and Picture Naming: Evidence for Asymmetric Connections between Bilingual Memory Representations. *Journal of Memory and Language* 33 (1994): 149–174.

Lambert, W.E., Tucker, G.R. & d'Anglejan, A. Cognitive and Attitudinal Consequences of Bilingual Schooling, *Journal of Educational Psychology* 85 (1973): 141–159.

Leach, P. *Your Baby and Child: From Birth to Age Five.* New York: Knopf, 1997.

Levy, E.S., Goral, M. & Obler, L.K. (in press). Doghouse/Chien Maison/Niche: Compounds in Bilinguals. In G. Libben ed., *Compounds.* Edmonton, Canada.

O'Mahoney, M. & Muhiudeen, H. A Preliminary Study of Alternative Taste Languages Using a Qualitative Description of Sodium Chloride Solutions: Malay Versus English. *British Journal of Psychology* 68 (1977): 275–278.

Peal, E. & Lambert, W.E. The Relation of Bilingualism to Intelligence. *Psychological Monographs: General and Applied* 76 (1962): 27, 1–3.

Tees, R.C. & Werker, J.F. (1984): (4), 579–590.

CHAPTER IV: BABIES LEARN TO TALK

Boysson-Bardies, B. de. *How Language Comes to Children.* (Translated by M.B. DeBevoise). Cambridge, Massachusetts: MIT Press, 1999.

Boysson-Bardies, B. de, Hallé, P., Sagart, L., & Durand, C. A. Cross-linguistic Investigation of Vowel Formants in Babbling. *Journal of Child Language* 16 (1989): 11–7.

Cairns, H. *The Acquisition of Language.* Austin, Texas: Pro-Ed., 1996.

DeCasper, A.J. & Spence, M.J. Prenatal Maternal Speech Influences Newborn's Perception of Speech Sounds. *Infant Behavior and Development* 9 (1986): 133–150.

Jusczyk, P.W., Hohne, E.A., & Mandel, D.R. Picking up Regularities in the Sound Structure of the Native Language. In Strange, W. ed., *Speech Perception and Linguistic Experience: Issues in Cross-language Research.* Timonium, Maryland, York Press, 1995.

Oller, D.K. The Emergence of the Sounds of Speech in Infancy. In Yeni-Komshian, Kavanagh, and Ferguson, *Child Phonology* 1 (1980).

Piaget, J. *The Origins of Intelligence in Children.* New York: International University Press, 1952.

Pinker, S. *The Language Instinct.* New York: Harper-Collins, 1994.

Polka, O. & Werker, J.F. Developmental Changes in Perception of Non-Native Vowel Contrasts. *Journal of Experimental Psychology: Human Perception and Performance* 20 (1994): 421–435.

Stark, R.E. Stages of Speech Development in the First Year of Life. In G. Yeni-Komshian, J. Kavanagh, and C.A. Ferguson eds., *Child Phonology, Vol. 1, Production.* New York: Academic Press, 1980.

Stoel-Gammon, C. The Phonological Skills of Two-year-olds. *Language, Speech and Hearing Services in Schools* 18 (1987): 323–329.

CHAPTER VI: THE SOUNDS OF SPANISH

Schnitzer, M.L. *Fonologia Contrastive: Española—Ingles*. San Juan, Puerto Rico: Piedras Press, 1997.

Index

Publisher's Acknowledgments

Special thanks to the Living Language team: Lisa Alpert, Elizabeth Bennett, Helen Tang, Elyse Tomasello, Christopher Warnasch, Suzanne McQuade, Pat Ehresmann, Marina Padakis, Denise DeGennaro, and Linda Schmidt.

About the Author

The author of this book, Erika Levy, is a researcher and multilingual practitioner of speech and language therapy, and an adjunct professor of linguistics. She holds an M.A. in Speech-Language Pathology. She grew up speaking French and English at home and learned the languages of the countries in which she lived.

More **LIVING LANGUAGE**® titles for **children!**

Learn Spanish Together
ISBN: 0-609-60210-1
$14.95/Canada $22.50

Learn Spanish Together: for the car*
ISBN: 0-609-60650-6
$14.95/Canada $22.50

Learn Spanish in the Kitchen*
ISBN: 0-609-60217-9
$18.95/Canada $26.50

Kids and grown-ups love our *Learn Together* series. Designed for children ages 4–8, these engaging activity kits teach basic Spanish words and phrases through games, songs, rhymes, and projects. Each kit includes a 48-page activity book, a 60-minute cassette, and 40 play-and-learn stickers.

*A 1998 Parents' Choice Award Winner

The *Learn Together* series is also available in French and Italian.

Available at your local bookstore or by calling 1-800-726-0600.
For a complete list of Living Language titles,
please visit our Web site at www.livinglanguage.com